LET'S-READ-AND-FIND-OUT SCIENCE

STAGE 2

Chirping CRICKETS

by Melvin Berger • illustrated by Megan Lloyd

HarperCollins*Publishers*

For Benjamin J., with love
—M.B.

For Cindy, Earl, and Michael
—M.L.

Special thanks to Marlene Zuk at the University of California at Riverside for her expert advice.

The illustrations in this book were done with watercolor and pen and ink on Saunders Waterford watercolor paper.

The *Let's-Read-and-Find-Out Science* book series was originated by Dr. Franklyn M. Branley, Astronomer Emeritus and former Chairman of the American Museum–Hayden Planetarium, and was formerly co-edited by him and Dr. Roma Gans, Professor Emeritus of Childhood Education, Teachers College, Columbia University. Text and illustrations for each of the books in the series are checked for accuracy by an expert in the relevant field. For more information about Let's-Read-and-Find-Out Science books, write to HarperCollins Children's Books, 195 Broadway, New York, NY 10007, or visit our web site at http://www.harperchildrens.com.

HarperCollins®, ❦®, and Let's Read-and-Find-Out Science® are trademarks of HarperCollins Publishers Inc.

Library of Congress Cataloging-in-Publication Data
Chirping crickets / by Melvin Berger ; illustrated by Megan Lloyd.
    p.   cm. — (Let's-read-and-find-out science. Stage 2)
Summary: Describes the physical characteristics, behavior, and life cycle of crickets while giving particular emphasis to how they chirp.
ISBN 0-06-024961-7. — ISBN 0-06-024962-5 (lib. bdg.).
ISBN 0-06-445180-1 (pbk.)
1. Crickets—Juvenile literature.   [1. Crickets.]   I. Lloyd, Megan, ill.   II. Title.   III. Series.
QL508.G8B47   1998
595.726—dc21   96-51661
                                                                        CIP
                                                                        AC

Chirping CRICKETS

It's late in the summer. The day is nearly over. The sun hangs low in the sky. Listen! The crickets are loudly chirping.

You can hear crickets chirping almost everywhere— in parks and woods, in fields and on lawns, along country roads, even inside your house.

It is the male crickets you hear. They usually stay in one spot and call the females to them. Most of the females cannot make sounds.

A male cricket does not chirp with his voice. He makes a chirping sound with his front wings. Each wing has a sharp edge called the scraper. The wing also has a long, bumpy vein called a file.

file

scraper

The cricket lifts up his front wings and rubs the scraper of one wing against the file of the other wing. *Chirp!* Back and forth he rubs his two front wings. *Chirp! Chirp! Chirp!*

Would you like to chirp like a male cricket? Get a piece of stiff paper and a nail file. Rub the file against the edge of the paper. The sound is almost the same as a cricket's chirp.

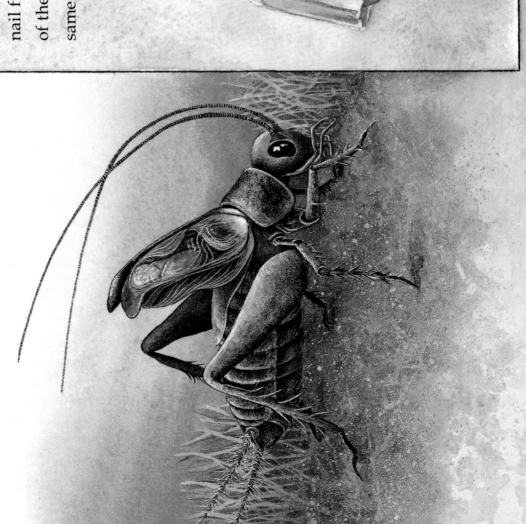

The "ears" of a cricket are not where you'd expect them to be. They are under the knees of the cricket's front legs! Each ear is a tiny hole with a tight, tissue-thin cover. Crickets hear chirping sounds through these tiny holes.

ear

ear

This is what happens: The chirps make the air move, or vibrate. The vibrating air forms sound waves. The sound waves spread out to all sides. When they bump into the cricket's ears, the cricket hears the sound.

A female cricket hears the male's chirps. She jumps toward the sound. Closer and closer she gets. Soon she is alongside the chirping male cricket, and they mate.

Inside the female, tiny eggs start to grow. When the eggs are ready, she uses a long, pointed tube at her back end to make tiny holes in the ground. Then she lays her eggs inside the holes. The eggs look like tiny yellow bananas.

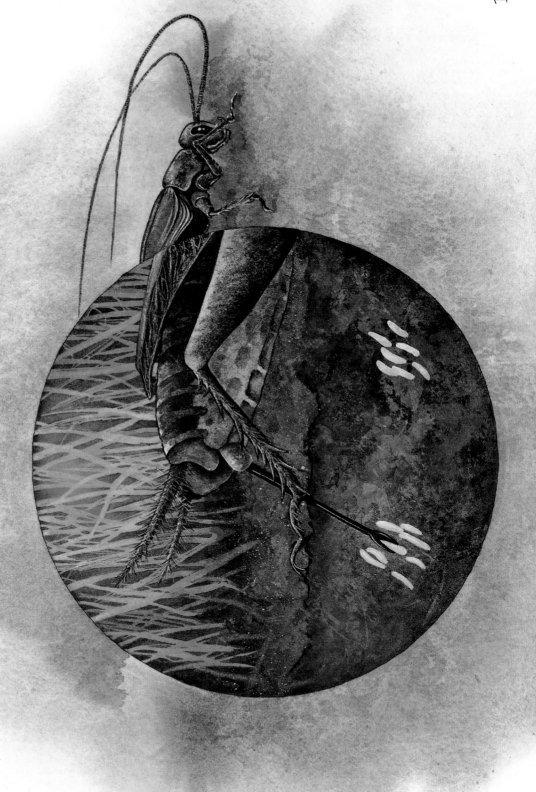

In the spring the eggs hatch into nymphs. A nymph is lighter in color than an adult cricket. It doesn't have any wings.

Soon the nymph gets too big for its hard outer covering. It wriggles out of its old skin and grows a new outside cover. This is called molting.

The nymphs molt again and again. Some nymphs molt as many as twelve times, depending on the amount of food available and the weather conditions. After the last molt they are adult crickets.

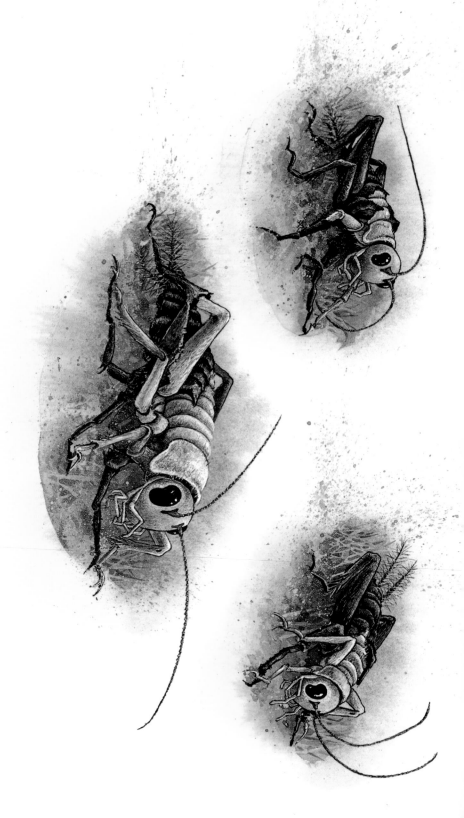

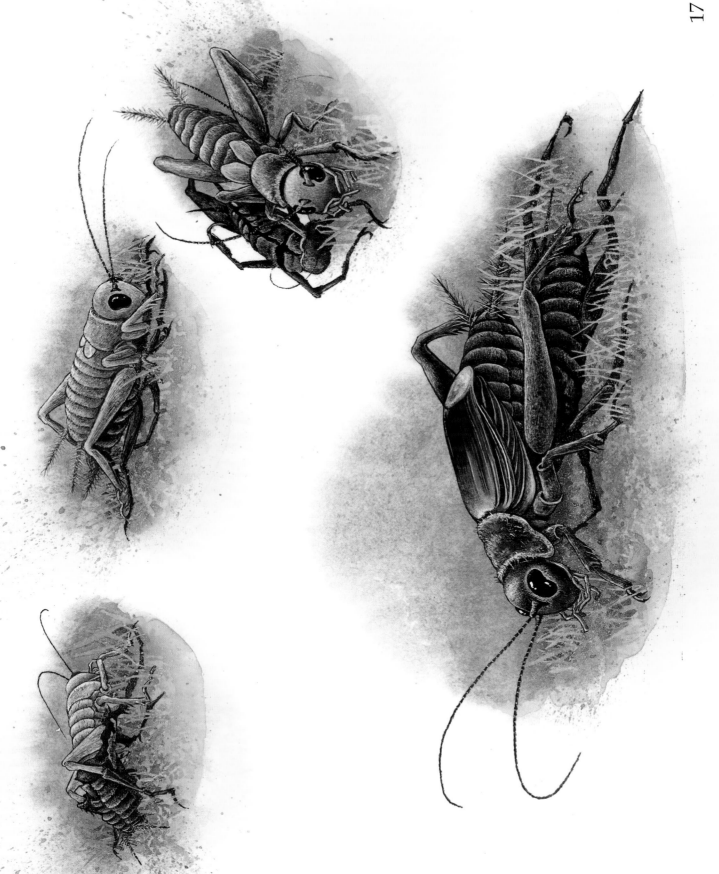

Most adult crickets have two pairs of wings—
front wings and back wings. Usually, the
wings lie flat over each other.
The back wings are bigger
than the front ones. Some
crickets use these for flying.
The front wings in males
are used to chirp.

back
wings

front
wings

Like all insects, crickets have three pairs of legs. The two front pairs are small. But the back legs are big and strong.

The cricket uses them when it jumps or flies away. Some crickets can leap as far as two feet. That's about as far as you can hop!

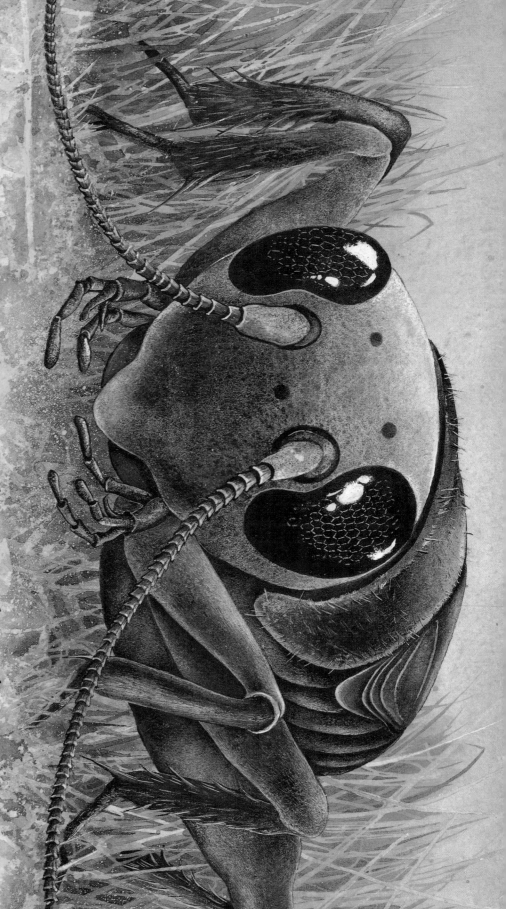

Crickets have two big eyes. Each eye is made up of many tiny eyes. They let the cricket see in many different directions at the same time, but a cricket's vision still isn't very good. In fact, crickets rely more on their ears to protect them from danger. Few enemies can sneak up on a cricket. You know that if you've ever tried to catch one.

The cricket's mouth is at the front of its head. It has no teeth. But its strong jaws are able to cut up the leaves and small insects it eats.

Two long, thin feelers on its head also help the cricket. These feelers are called antennae. Some antennae are longer than the cricket's whole body. Antennae help crickets find food and alert them to danger.

Thousands of different kinds of crickets live around the world. **Field crickets** are the most common. They are about one inch long and are dark brown or black in color. Field crickets mostly live in tiny tunnels in the ground.

Male field crickets sit in their tunnel entrances all day and chirp loudly at night. At the same time, they are watching out for danger. If an enemy shows up, the male field cricket gives a high, piping chirp. Into the tunnel he pops.

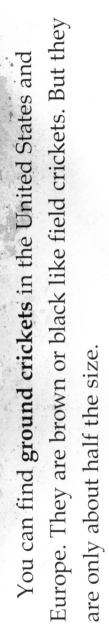

You can find **ground crickets** in the United States and Europe. They are brown or black like field crickets. But they are only about half the size.

Ground crickets settle in damp places such as grassy riverbanks. Their song sounds like the tinkling of bells.

Many ground crickets hide during the daylight hours. But at night they are active—eating, fighting, and mating.

Tree crickets are the same size as field crickets. But they are pale green or white in color. Their very long antennae reach back to the tips of their rear legs.

Male tree crickets do not usually chirp alone. Instead, they chirp in groups. A typical chorus of tree crickets may have hundreds of males. Their high-pitched song sounds like "*Treet-treet-treet.*"

Tree crickets hide in trees, bushes, and tall grass. Here they find the smaller insects that they like to eat.

House crickets are best known in Europe. They would rather live indoors, especially in warm places. Their favorite spots are near a stove, fireplace, or heater. These light-brown or yellow crickets endlessly repeat their high, trilling sound. Many people believe that house crickets bring good luck. Having a cricket in your house, they say, means that nice things will happen to you.

The sky is very dark now. The loud chirpings of the crickets fill the air. It is the nighttime sound of late summer.

YOUR PET CRICKET

It's fun to catch and study a pet cricket for a while. Find a big, clean jar or clear plastic container with a wide neck and a cover. Put an inch of dirt in the jar. Ask an adult to poke lots of small holes in the cover so that the cricket can breathe.

Take your jar outdoors late some afternoon near the end of summer. Walk around until you hear the sound of a chirping cricket. Gently tap the cricket into the jar. Then screw on the cover.

At home, open the jar and drop in some food. Crickets will eat bits of lettuce or banana, moist bread, a drop of honey, or even dry dog or cat food. It's good to add an egg-carton-cup shelter, because crickets usually don't chirp unless they feel safe, knowing they have somewhere to hide. Watch your cricket jump around and eat the food. Listen for its chirps.

Enjoy your cricket for a day and then let it go. Put it back where you found it. Crickets don't like to be in cages. They need their freedom, the same as you and I do.

TELLING THE TEMPERATURE

Did you know that tree crickets can tell us the temperature? The warmer it is, the faster they chirp. In cooler weather, their chirps slow down.

Try this the next time you hear a chirping cricket. Get a watch with a second hand. Count the number of chirps the cricket makes in 15 seconds. How many chirps did you hear—10? 15? 20? 25?

Add 40 to this number. Let's say you heard 20 chirps. The temperature is 20 + 40, or 60 degrees Fahrenheit.

FIND OUT MORE ABOUT CRICKETS

- MAKE A CRICKET MODEL

  Items needed:

  3 joined egg carton sections   6 pipe cleaners

  1 marker   1 sheet of construction paper

  1. Refer to the crickets in this book as you build your model.
  2. Do *not* separate the egg carton sections. The first section of the egg carton will be the cricket's head, the second its thorax, and the third its abdomen.
  3. On the head, draw two eyes and mouthparts.
  4. Attach two pipe cleaners to the head for antennae.
  5. Poke one pipe cleaner through the front area of the thorax for the two front legs. Repeat a bit farther back for the two middle legs. Last, use one pipe cleaner apiece for the long back legs.
  6. Cut both the larger (back) and smaller (front) wings out of construction paper and tape them to the upper front area of the thorax.

  Now you've made your own cricket!

- JUMP LIKE A CRICKET

  With masking tape, tape a six-foot-long line on the floor. Mark off two-foot segments. Jump from one mark to the next. You are jumping the same distance that a cricket jumps.

- PLAY A "DO YOU KNOW?" GAME

  Do you know that a cricket has six legs?
  Can you name another animal with: six legs? more than six legs? fewer than six legs?
  Do you know that a cricket is about one inch long?
  Can you name another animal that is: one inch long? bigger than one inch long? smaller than one inch long?
  Do you know that a cricket makes music?
  Can you name another animal that makes music? Can you make the sound?
  Do you know that a cricket has two antennae?
  Can you name another animal that: has two antennae? has no antennae?